Images of Western Newfoundland
A Photographic Journey

text and photographs by
Keith Nicol

Images of Western Newfoundland

BREAKWATER

Breakwater
100 Water Street
P.O. Box 2188
St. John's, Newfoundland
A1C 6E6

Also by Keith Nicol
Best Hiking Trails in Western Newfoundland

The Publisher gratefully acknowledges the financial support of The Canada Council, which has helped make this publication possible.

The Publisher acknowledges the financial support of the Cultural Affairs Division of the Department of Municipal and Provincial Affairs, Government of Newfoundland and Labrador, which has made this publication possible.

Canadian Cataloguing in Publication Data

Nicol, Keith

  Images of western Newfoundland
  ISBN 0-920911-88-9

1. Newfoundland -- Description and travel --
1981 -- Views. * I. Title.

FC2195.W47N52   1990   971-804'0222   C90-097633-0
F1124.W47N52   1990

Dedication

To my mother, Marjorie, my wife, Heather, and Mike
Fretwell, whose spirit of adventure lives in us all.

Introduction

Newfoundland sits at the eastern end of the Gulf of St. Lawrence like a shield, protecting the other Maritime provinces from the windswept fury of the Atlantic Ocean. Jutting out into the cold Labrador current, its forests and wildlife have a subarctic appearance very different from the other Atlantic provinces. Newfoundland's terrain is distinct, the product of continents colliding and then being wrenched apart by enormous subterranean forces. These processes have produced a rugged and beautiful land, where many people still live in small 'outports' strung along the sea.

Newfoundland and Labrador is large (405,720 square kilometres or 156,648 square miles); it is three times larger than Nova Scotia, New Brunswick and Prince Edward Island combined. The coastlines of the Island and Labrador span an incredible 17,540 kilometres (10,900 miles), more than twice the distance across Canada. Although the province of Newfoundland is known for its maritime environment, it has several mountain ranges, including the Torngat Range in Labrador, which include the highest peaks east of the

Rockies. The province is also dissected by a multitude of lakes, ponds and rivers. Therefore, it is not surprising to find distinctly different regions within Newfoundland. But perhaps none is more impressive than that region found along the west coast of the island of Newfoundland and in southern Labrador.

Connecting this west coast region like a backbone are the Long Range Mountains, which include the Island's highest point, Lewis Hills. The major attraction in this region is Gros Morne National Park, which is Atlantic Canada's newest and largest national park. Recently, Gros Morne received worldwide recognition for its spectacular and distinctive landscape by being added to UNESCO's prestigious list of World Heritage sites. This region also includes two historic sites of international acclaim: the Basque whaling station at Red Bay, Labrador; and the Viking site at L'Anse aux Meadows, Newfoundland. The Viking site is of special importance, because it is the earliest documented discovery of European settlement in North

America. It has also been proclaimed a UNESCO World Heritage site and, together with Gros Morne Park, joins areas of global importance like the Galapagos Islands, the Great Barrier Reef of Australia and the Pyramids of Egypt.

Port aux Basques lies at the southern end of this west coast region, and the Trans Canada Highway heads north along the base of the Long Range Mountains past Stephenville to Corner Brook, the region's largest community. From there, the only major gap in the Long Range Mountains occurs at Deer Lake. The Viking Trail, Highway 430, branches off the Trans Canada Highway at this point and traverses the Northern Peninsula parallel to the Long Range Mountains, ending at St. Anthony. Southern Labrador has also been included in this region, because it can only be accessed by ferry from St. Barbe on the Northern Peninsula, and because it has many economic and cultural links with the Island's western region.

Western Newfoundland is also one of North America's last areas of accessible, untouched wilderness. Although it has had a long history of settlement ever since the Vikings landed at L'Anse aux Meadows roughly 1000 years ago, this part of the province is still awaiting discovery. It is a land of surprises, from sand dunes to rugged mountains; from fjords which rival the ones in Norway to unusual 'moonscapes,' which look more like an Arizona desert than a wilderness area in Atlantic Canada. Western Newfoundland lays claim to a multitude of lakes, or 'ponds,' and each year, salmon negotiate countless numbers of brooks and streams. Today, visitors travelling to western Newfoundland and southern Labrador can combine superb hiking or canoeing with photography and wildlife viewing. They can see where the Basque whalers created the province's first 'oil boom,' or where the first Europeans, the Vikings, lived in North America. With proper management of this natural and human heritage, the legends of the past and the wilderness of today may be preserved as an inheritance for all who may visit this land tomorrow.

Valley of Contrasts, Gros Morne National Park

Bottle Cove, Bay of Islands

Stream near Port aux Basques

1

The Land and Sea

The Long Range Mountains

Newfoundland's mountains provide both striking scenery and an insight into how the island of Newfoundland was formed. The Long Range Mountains, from which numerous streams and rivers flow in all directions, are the spine of western Newfoundland. But these mountains are different from others in Canada. Names like Table Mountain and the Tablelands accurately describe their appearance. They are old mountains, greatly reshaped from their previous, more dramatic forms, by water, wind and ice.

The Long Range Mountains may have taken shape when the continents of Europe and North America collided four to five hundred million years ago. Geologists now know that the continents slowly moved across the earth's surface, driven by convection currents in its semi-molten interior. When these continents came together, land was folded and thrusted up, creating whole mountain ranges in the process. Pieces of the ocean floor were even pushed onto the earth's surface. This was the case in western Newfoundland, where remnants of several slices of the ocean's floor and sub-floor have been found on the mountain tops. The continents of North America and Europe were then wrenched apart, creating the Atlantic Ocean, leaving behind the Appalachian Mountains in the United States and the Long Range Mountains in western Newfoundland.

Initially, the Long Range Mountains may have resembled the present Rocky Mountains, but over time they have lost their impressive grandeur. Subsequent ice ages carved knife-like gouges in the weaker rocks, producing western Newfoundland's dramatic slopes and valleys. Today, the mountain range stretches 450 kilometres (279 miles) from Port aux Basques to the end of the Northern Peninsula, with its highest point (822 metres, 2673 feet) in the Lewis Hills.

Western Newfoundland's Rivers, Lakes and Ponds

In combination with abundant precipitation, the rocky spine created by the Long Range Mountains has produced countless water courses that flow off its mountain slopes. There are approximately 90 streams and 20 lakes, or ponds, in western Newfoundland and southern Labrador. Because the Long Range Mountains are so close to the sea, most of the streams are small in size. The only exception is the Humber River, which breaches the Long Range Mountains at Corner Brook. It is western Newfoundland's only large river and, at 125 miles (201 kilometres) in length, is the second largest river on the Island. The Pinware in southern Labrador is the largest river along that section of coast.

What western Newfoundland lacks in long rivers, it compensates for in spectacular lakes. It is probable that glacial ice poured out of the Long Range Mountains on several occasions, and the results are the fjord-like lakes so abundant in this area. Grand Lake, the largest lake on the Island, was deepened in this way, as were the dramatic sequence of lakes found in Gros Morne National Park, including Ten Mile Pond and Western Brook Pond. Here, walled-in by sheer rock 600 metres (2000 feet) high, are some of eastern Canada's most impressive lakes—one of the reasons Gros Morne National Park is now world famous.

The Coastline of Western Newfoundland

The coastline of western Newfoundland is as varied as its upland terrain. Long, sandy beaches extend in swaths from Port aux Basques to southern Labrador. Some shoreline is backed by low-lying agricultural fields. Other shoreline areas have abrupt cliffs extending over 500 feet (152 metres) high, where sea stacks and sea caves provide silent reminders of the eroding effects of the ocean waves.

Like the Long Range Mountains and river valleys, western Newfoundland's shore zone has also been scraped and scoured by glaciers. The Bay of Islands and Bonne Bay, long time favourites of early fishermen because of their protected waters, owe this protection to the movement of glaciers so many centuries ago. In fact, these two inlets are the only large areas featuring protected waters along the entire west coast.

Flora and Fauna of Western Newfoundland

In many respects, the forests of western Newfoundland are more like those in the Yukon than those in the other Atlantic provinces. Newfoundland is bathed by the cool Labrador current, which produces a subarctic boreal kind of forest composed of black spruce, balsam fir, white spruce and white birch. In windswept areas, these trees often take on a stunted and contorted form. The scientific name for this vegetation form is *Krummholz*, meaning 'bent stick' in German. In Newfoundland, the word *tuckamore* is used to describe this almost impenetrable mass of branches and needles.

Bogs are common in much of the low-lying land, and it is in these bogs that larch, one of the few coniferous trees which drops its needles in the fall, may be found among other 'bog plants.' One of the most interesting bog plants is the carnivorous pitcher plant, Newfoundland's provincial flower. This plant manufactures a sweet perfume to attract insects, which then slide down the fine slippery hairs within the 'pitcher' and become trapped. Enzymes produced by the plant dissolve the insect, thus providing nutrients not available in the soil in which it grows. The insect-eating sundew is another plant which has converted predators into prey. The sundew is much smaller than the pitcher plant, however, so a keen eye is required to pick it out amidst the other bog plants.

At higher altitudes and in windswept areas along the coast, tundra or 'barren ground' vegetation is found. In order to survive, plants in these environments take on a dwarfed or cushion-like appearance. Lichens, mosses, dwarf willows and birches frequent this zone. Insect-eating sundews and butter-worts can also be found in many tundra areas.

Although Newfoundland's boreal forest is not known for its autumn foliage, large areas of birch, combined with the occasional red maple and mountain ash, produce delightful fall colours. The most brilliant fall colours in Newfoundland can be found in the Humber Valley, and on the slopes surrounding Corner Brook.

Generally, the underlying bedrock seems to have had a minimal impact on the vegetation in most of western Newfoundland. A striking exception occurs where peridotite is found. This bedrock has low levels of calcium and high concentrations of chromium, nickel and magnesium, which tend to be toxic to most plants. Outcrops of peridotite occur in the Lewis Hills, Blow-me-down (Blomidon) Mountains, the North Arm Mountains and on the Tablelands in Gros Morne National Park, and they have resulted in a 'moonscape' which provides a remarkable contrast to the adjacent forested slopes. Despite the general lack of vegetation, some plants—including the pitcher plant, the larch, the common juniper, and several flowers—have adapted to the unusual chemistry that the presence of peridotite has caused.

The diversity of fauna in the western portion of Newfoundland reflects the sub arctic climate, vegetation cover, and island setting. These factors explain why numerous animals common to Nova Scotia and Labrador are not found here; in fact, only 14 indigenous species of mammals are found on the Island. Examples include the beaver, red fox, black bear, arctic hare and caribou. Moose were introduced in 1878; there are now over 70,000 of them. Surprisingly, there are no indigenous amphibians or reptiles found on the Island.

In contrast, Newfoundland has a varied bird population. Two hundred and twenty-seven species of birds have been recorded. Of particular interest in western Newfoundland are the fish-catching osprey, the bald eagle, the willow ptarmigan and the cheerful black-capped chickadee.

Western Newfoundland's rivers, lakes and streams are known for the quality fishing they provide, not for the diversity of fish stocks in them, as only fish requiring cold, clear water can survive in these waters. An angler can catch with ease the posted limit of Atlantic salmon, rainbow trout, eastern brook trout (or speckled trout) and landlocked salmon, with the unusual name of *ouananiche*. Although Atlantic salmon stocks seem to have slipped recently, several river enhancement projects in western Newfoundland are attempting to reverse that trend. Any visitor to Big Falls on the Humber River from mid-June to mid-July is almost certain to be thrilled by watching Atlantic salmon attempt to leap the 3 metre (10 foot) falls.

Blue Ponds, Near Corner Brook

'The Arches,' Northern Peninsula

Margaret Bowater Park, Corner Brook

Torrent River, Northern Peninsula

Windswept vegetation, locally called tuckamore

A pond near Deer Lake

2

Western Newfoundland Outdoors

Western Newfoundland and southern Labrador are ideally suited to outdoor recreational activities. The terrain in this area combines with the climate to provide unlimited opportunities for summer and fall hiking, canoeing, ocean kayaking, fishing, hunting and nature photography. In the winter, it can offer superb cross-country and alpine skiing. Newfoundland will appeal to outdoor enthusiasts who enjoy the challenges nature has to offer, who thrill at seeing wildlife in their natural habitat, and who obtain personal satisfaction and a sense of well-being from being in the wilderness.

Long known as a hunting and fishing paradise, western Newfoundland can provide hours of satisfaction for fly fishermen testing their skills against the famed Atlantic salmon, or hunters trying for trophy caribou or moose. However, with the recent interest across North America in fitness-related outdoor activities such as hiking, canoeing and cross-country skiing, the tremendous potential of western Newfoundland is just beginning to be recognized.

The rivers that provide clear water for spawning salmon can also deliver a superb white water canoeing experience, and the mountains that are home to the caribou are ideal for hiking or cross-country skiing.

Lakes, Ponds, Rivers

Most of the lakes in western Newfoundland are located on the Northern Peninsula, along the flat coastal plain that parallels the western shoreline. However, visitors should realize that the Newfoundland term *pond* doesn't necessarily mean a small lake, since Western Brook Pond in Gros Morne National Park is 16 kilometres long and 150 metres deep. Of all the lakes in western Newfoundland, Western Brook Pond is the most impressive. A boat trip to the end of the pond (operating three times a day from June to mid-September) would be the highlight of any tourist's visit. Its fjord-like setting and crystal clear water make it one of the most photogenic lakes in eastern Canada.

The Humber River has its headwaters in the high country of the Long Range Mountains. From Matty's Pond, located just a few kilometres south of Western Brook Pond, the Humber River falls 470 metres (1525 feet) in 213 kilometres (128 miles) to the ocean in Corner Brook. The Humber is probably best known for its prolific salmon run, and up to 4000 salmon are caught by anglers every summer. The river also provides good canoeing along many of its lower sections. Big Falls on the Humber River is within the boundaries of Sir Richard Squires Provincial Park, and during the main salmon run in late June and early July, the Falls is a popular fishing and photography spot. Salmon can be seen jumping along the entire 87 metre (282 foot) length of the falls. Although few salmon are successful in leaping the 3 metre (10 foot) falls, they can swim up the fish ladder which was blasted out of the rock on the right bank of the river. Below Big Falls, the Humber River flows through Deer Lake just before emptying into the ocean. The forested valley slopes and smooth waters of the lower reaches of the Humber can provide a picturesque canoeing experience for the novice or intermediate paddler.

In contrast, the Main River will appeal to the expert canoeist. Located at the base of the Northern Peninsula, the Main River flows from the heart of the Long Range Mountains eastward to the tidewater at Sop's Arm. Since it was ranked by Parks Canada as one of the top ten wilderness rivers in the country, the Main River has received national recognition. Its attractions include abundant wildlife, excellent salmon fishing and challenging canoeing. Although it is only 55 kilometres (33 miles) long, the arduousness of the journey means that paddlers should plan to spend five to seven days on the river.

Long Range Mountains

The Long Range Mountains stand out like a giant platform above the surrounding coastal plain. Because they are relatively flat on top, hiking on them is a safe and enjoyable way to explore many sections of the mountain range. Hiking trails exist on the Table Mountains near Port aux Basques; the Lewis Hills near Stephenville; the Blow-me-down Mountains near Corner Brook; the Tablelands near Woody Point; and the Gros Morne and Long Range Mountains near Rocky Harbour. Of these, the most spectacular trails are probably those in the Blow-me-down Mountains, where there are breathtaking views of the island-studded Bay of Islands. However, the most popular trail is the trek up Gros Morne, the mountain for which Gros Morne National Park is named.

These mountains are also excellent for ski touring in the winter and spring. The Long Range Mountains receive more snow (over 400 centimetres or 160 inches) than any place on the Island. In many locations, cross-country skiing usually begins in mid-December and extends into mid-May. The most popular area for ski touring is the Blow-me-down Mountains near Corner Brook, where the combination of reliable snow cover and stunning ocean vistas make it one of the best areas for ski touring this side of the Alberta Rockies. The uninitiated should realize, however, that 'Blow-me-down' is a term which aptly describes the winter weather in these mountains. Since winter storms develop rapidly, few skiers venture into the Blow-me-downs during January and February. The preferred time for skiing in this area is March, April and May, when the weather is sunniest and the snow is softer.

With the exception of the occasional ski trip into the Long Range Mountains near Gros Morne National Park, most of the higher mountains on the west coast remain uncharted in terms of ski touring. The cross-country skiing on the Lewis

Hills near Stephenville, or the Table Mountains near Port aux Basques, is superb in late winter and early spring, but few people ever venture into these areas.

Marble Mountain

The only alpine ski area in western Newfoundland and southern Labrador, Marble Mountain is located on a north facing slope along the slopes of the Humber Valley. It has been recognized as the best ski area in Atlantic Canada, and one of the top four or five in Canada. One writer said that "it is the best skiing between Banff, Alberta and Val d'Isere, France." Served by several lifts, including a one-mile-long double chairlift, Marble Mountain has become a major ski destination in Atlantic Canada. The most popular time to visit Marble Mountain is during the last week in February, which coincides with the Corner Brook Winter Carnival. Torchlight parades, ski racing competitions, cross-country ski tours, snow sculpture contests and many other events designed to celebrate western Newfoundland's long winter are making the Carnival a major winter tourist attraction.

The Coastline of Western Newfoundland

Near Port aux Basques and Cow Head, wide sandy beaches provide ideal natural hiking routes. These are the most extensive beaches in western Newfoundland; individual beaches are as long as 7 kilometres (4.2 miles). As well, there are many shorter sections of sandy beach which can be found throughout the coast and in southern Labrador.

In contrast to these smooth, sandy beaches, the rest of the coastline on the west coast is composed of rock and cliffs. While this type of shore is spectacular to look at, it is difficult to traverse. Fortunately, there are some magnificent routes for hikers interested in coastal trails, the most impressive being the trail between Cape St. George and Mainland on the Port au Port Peninsula. This route traverses the most scenic shore in western Newfoundland, and offers breathtaking views of the Gulf of St. Lawrence.

Another dramatic vantage point is near Bottle Cove in the Bay of Islands. From an elevation of 1000 feet (305 metres), the view into the blue-green waters of Bottle Cove appears almost tropical. The Green Garden Trail in Gros Morne National Park offers a different coastline experience, since this route cuts through a smooth, grassy terrace which overlooks the sea. Here, pillow lavas formed from undersea lava flow, sea stacks and sea caves give the hiker ample opportunities to explore.

Much of the western side of the Northern Peninsula is similar, with mile after mile of gravel and cobble beaches surrounded, in most areas, by low cliffs. In contrast, the Peninsula's eastern shore is rugged, steep and accessible (for the most part) only by boat.

Western Newfoundland's coastline has evolved over long periods of time, and its diverse character is due in measure to the wind, waves and ice. This has produced a striking shoreline which begs to be explored, either on foot or by ocean kayak.

Marina at Corner Brook

Tablelands, Gros Morne National Park

Marble Mountain, near Corner Brook

From Blow-me-down Mountains towards Humber Arm

Near Western Brook Pond, Gros Morne National Park

3

Gros Morne National Park

Gros Morne is Atlantic Canada's newest and largest national park. Its beauty has long been recognized and inspired author Harold Horwood to write, "There is nothing like it east of the Rockies or south of Labrador." But Gros Morne is more than scenic mountains and fjords. On June 10, 1988, in a ceremony presided over by Britain's Prince Edward, Gros Morne became Canada's newest World Heritage Site. Its significance was explained by then-federal Minister of the Environment, Tom McMillan: "What the Galapagos Islands are to the biological sciences, Gros Morne National Park is to geology." For just as the Galapagos Islands present compelling support for evolution and species development—the basis for modern biology—Gros Morne National Park provides clear evidence of plate tectonics or continental drift—the basis for modern geology.

One of the most interesting aspects of continental drift exposed in Gros Morne National Park is the moonscape-like Tablelands, located in the southern section of the Park. The visual effect of this area is startling: a barren orange-coloured mountain surrounded by a sea of green spruce and fir. The Tablelands capture the attention and curiosity of all who see them, but what has caused this apparent desert in the midst of a spruce and fir forest?

Historic Collision

The Tablelands owe their dramatic influence on vegetation to a rock called peridotite. The origins of peridotite date to ancient times and are the result of the collision of the two continents. It is known that the Tablelands were once part of the floor of the Atlantic Ocean, and were pushed atop western Newfoundland when Europe and North America collided millions of years ago.

Dr. Doug Grant of the Geological Survey of Canada has been visiting Gros Morne for the past 20 years. He explains: "The short answer for lack of vegetation is that plant life on the earth has adapted to soil conditions derived from surface rocks. Peridotite comes from the mantle and is a foreign material for most plants. Specifically, the rock is very low in calcium, very high in magnesium and has toxic amounts of heavy metals, so few plants can grow in it."

"The landscape of Gros Morne National Park is not only interesting from a continental drift viewpoint, but is equally spectacular in terms of more recent glaciations," says Dave Huddlestone, the Park's former Chief of Visitors' Services. "Most of the spectacular scenery in the Park, like the steep cliffs bounding Western Brook Pond or Ten Mile Pond, is the result of large amounts of glacial ice pouring out of the Long Range Mountains over the past 100,000 years. But you certainly don't need a Ph.D. in geology to appreciate the beauty of those areas." It is because of that spectacular beauty and for what the rocks have revealed about continental drift and glaciation that the Park was chosen as a World Heritage Site.

More Than Rocks

Of course, there is more to Gros Morne National Park than the story told within its rocks. Gros Morne's coastal environment, its forested coastal plain, its valley slopes and mountain tops are home to 750 plant species, many at the extreme ranges of their distribution. These plants provide food and shelter for 19 species of land mammals and 230 bird species. As well, just offshore, there are 15 types of marine mammals, including whales and seals.

Within the Park's boundary, a 5000 year human history has been traced, a history which continues in the numerous fishing villages found adjacent to the Park today. Scenes of fishermen hauling lobster traps, gathering hay from a local meadow, or salting freshly caught cod are commonplace, epitomizing for many visitors western Newfoundland's unique and special culture.

The outdoor recreational activities presented by the diverse water and land environments attract tens of thousands of people to the Park annually. Besides sight-seeing and camping, the Park has nearly 70 kilometres (44 miles) of maintained hiking trails. Of particular interest is the James Callaghan Trail, which ascends Gros Morne mountain. For the experienced backpacker, the high country off the beaten path offers unlimited hiking in an arctic-alpine setting. It is within this high elevation zone that wildlife sightings, particularly of moose, caribou and arctic hare, are likely. The latter two are especially interesting, since they are normally found much further north. The numerous rivers, lakes and the inshore ocean waters near the Park provide opportunities for canoeing, ocean kayaking and fishing. In winter, the Park takes on a snowy cloak to provide enthusiasts opportunities for cross-country skiing and snow-shoeing.

Toward Lobster Cove Lighthouse

Cow Head

Rocky Harbour Pond and Gros Morne Mountain

Sunset at Rocky Harbour

Lobster Cove Lighthouse

Cow Head Beach

4

Port au Choix
and L'Anse aux Meadows

The Maritime Archaic Indians

A building excavation in the community of Port au Choix in 1967 led to a chance discovery of a major burial site belonging to the Maritime Archaic Indians, a people who lived along the west coast of Newfoundland between 3200 and 4300 years ago.

The excavated skeletons show that these Indians were robust and strong. From artifacts discovered in the burial site, it is known they lived off the resources from the sea, not by agriculture. Their very name indicates this: 'maritime' denotes a reliance on the ocean, while 'archaic' means that they are an old or historic culture. They appear to have used stone axes, and small knives made from beaver teeth or antler handles were common. One knife found at Port au Choix resembles a 'crooked knife' or amulet used by many northern people today. Their clothing seems to have been sewn with fine needles, probably fashioned from small bird bones. Judging from the beads, rows of shells and small bones present, every effort seems to have been made to decorate their clothing.

Although less can be discerned about the spiritual side of their culture, burials appear to have been elaborate. Red ochre powder was sprinkled over many bodies, and the tools and ornaments frequently found in graves suggest a belief that life after death was similar to worldly life.

Dorset Eskimos

Although Dorset Eskimo artifacts have not been found at the site in Port au Choix, they have been discovered nearby at Cape Riche. In the early 1960s, in an area known as Phillips Garden, evidence of an early Eskimo settlement that existed between 1500 and 2200 years ago was excavated.

These people appear to have lived in houses of rock and earth during the winter and in tents along the ocean throughout the summer. Like their predecessors, the Maritime Archaic Indians, they would have hunted, fished and eaten wild foods like seasonal berries. Because they wintered and summered along the coast, they probably relied more on the sea than the Maritime Archaic Indians. It is not known if they lived in snow houses, but they did not use dog sleds, an important aspect of modern Eskimo culture. Since only one grave was located, little is known of their religious beliefs and burial practices.

Both the Dorset Eskimos and Maritime Archaic Indians disappeared from Newfoundland, and no one knows what became of them. Disease or the failure of an important fishery or sea harvest may have taken its toll. At any rate, 3000 years ago the Maritime Archaic Indians disappeared completely from the Canadian east coast, followed 1700 years later by the Dorset Eskimos.

Port aux Choix Today

Today, Parks Canada has a Visitors' Centre with displays and artifacts of both the Maritime Archaic Indians and Dorset Eskimos. The Centre is located in Port au Choix, adjacent to the field where the Archaic Indian site is located. This site is several kilometres from Phillips Garden.

Also worth visiting is the Pointe Riche Lighthouse, located a few kilometres from Port au Choix. The lighthouse is the starting point for a 3.5 kilometre (2 mile) scenic coastal hike. Port au Choix is 220 kilometres (120 miles) from Deer Lake, where Highway 430 begins.

L'Anse aux Meadows

L'Anse aux Meadows is located at the northern tip of Newfoundland's Great Northern Peninsula. In 1960, the community had no roads and was home to just three families. However, soon this would change. When he first began researching the area, Norwegian explorer and writer Helge Ingstad asked resident George Decker if he knew of any unusual foundations or house sites that would have pre-dated the earliest residents of L'Anse aux Meadows. Decker directed Ingstad to an area adjacent to Epaves Bay, where faint outlines of what appeared to be ancient foundations were overgrown with tall grass and weeds. When Ingstad asked Mr. Decker if he knew who had occupied those buildings, George Decker said, "No one knows. They were here before the fishermen came to L'Anse aux Meadows...and my family was the first to settle here." On the basis of this information, Ingstad began the archaeological dig that was to change forever the way historians documented the early exploration of North America.

The Vikings

The Vikings from Norway, Sweden and Denmark were remarkable explorers and colonizers of new lands. Accounts of these explorations were eventually recorded in the *Sagas*. Of particular interest is the thirteenth-century *Greenlander's Saga* which describes the travels of Leif Eiriksson and Bjarni Herjolfsson. In 986 A.D., Bjarni Herjolfsson was blown off course in poor weather while on a trip from Iceland to Greenland. He reported that when the skies cleared, he could see a low-lying coastline covered with trees. He had never seen a land like this and knew it could not be Greenland, so he sailed northeast until he reached the familiar shores of Greenland. His reports of this new land convinced Leif Eiriksson to search for it, and in 1001 A.D., together with some of Bjarni Herjolfsson's crew, he set sail for the uncharted sea that lay to the west. The *Sagas* tell of Leif Eiriksson's sighting of a low, forested land rimmed with long, white, sandy beaches. He sailed south for two more days until he came to an area of lush, grassy meadows. The land was rich and the sea bountiful, and this encouraged Leif Eiriksson and his crew to spend the winter. One day, a crew member reportedly found grapes growing there, and it is believed that this is why Leif Eiriksson named this new land Winlandia or Vinland, Land of the Wine. They built 'large houses,' fished for salmon and cut timber, which was especially valuable, since in Greenland suitable timber for building was scarce. The next summer they returned to Greenland and their success triggered a series of visits to 'Vinland' by the Vikings.

One expedition was led by Icelandic trader Thor Finn Karlsefni, and he arrived at Lief's camp with 160 people, including 15 women. They obviously intended to stay for some time since they brought livestock to produce milk, meat and wool. The *Sagas* report that initial relationships with the natives or 'Skraelings' were friendly, but they eventually deteriorated and clashes soon broke out between the two groups. This forced Thor Finn Karlsefni to return to Greenland with his wife and their child Snorri, the first European born in the New World. It appears that subsequent expeditions to Vinland were very sporadic, often hampered by storms and poor weather. Eventually, buildings in Vinland decayed and grassy meadows reclaimed the ground on which the Vikings had lived.

Is L'Anse aux Meadows Winlandia?

While it is clear that the Vikings were the first Europeans to live in North America—a full five centuries before Christopher Columbus set foot in the New World—an important question is still unresolved. Is the site at L'Anse aux Meadows the Vinland of the Norse *Sagas*? The principle argument against this claim is that the wild grapes from which most wine is made could not have grown in L'Anse aux Meadows because it would have been simply too cold for the grapes to have survived. Arguments supporting the fact that this site is Vinland refute this by suggesting that Leif Eiriksson mistakenly referred to blueberries, which are abundant at L'Anse aux Meadows, as grapes. Other archaeologists suggest that the name Vinland was chosen to create the impression of a favourable settlement site. After all, the Norse had named an island of rock and ice Greenland, probably for a similar reason. If this site is not Vinland, then L'Anse aux Meadows was probably a 'gateway' community, a place where the Vikings refitted their boats prior to sailing for Greenland.

Although the debate concerning the exact location of Leif Eiriksson's Vinland may never be resolved, the significance of the discovery of a European settlement at L'Anse aux Meadows is, nevertheless, exciting. Because of Helge Ingstad's work, L'Anse aux Meadows was the first Canadian site to be named to UNESCO's prestigious World Heritage list. A UNESCO plaque placed at L'Anse aux Meadows reads:

> L'Anse aux Meadows is the first authenticated Norse site in North America. Its sod buildings are thus the earliest known European structures on this continent; its smithy, the site of the first known iron workings in the New World; the site itself the scene of the first known conflicts between native Americans and Europeans. It is therefore one of the world's major archaeological sites.

L'Anse aux Meadows Today

Since the discovery of a Viking settlement at L'Anse aux Meadows in 1960, Parks Canada has recreated a portion of the eleventh-century Viking settlement. From the faint foundation outline, Parks Canada reconstructed three sod buildings similar to the kind the Vikings built in Greenland

and Iceland 1000 years ago. Excavations within the foundations of eight other house sites have revealed that the Vikings were surprisingly organized. One collection of buildings was used to build and repair ships. From the large amount of wood and debris unearthed at another site, it is clear that this is where the carpenters lived and worked. Most significant is the set of three buildings near Black Duck Brook, which provided living and working quarters for the iron smiths. Here they roasted bog iron-ore, which was then smelted in a furnace. Charcoal would have been used to produce the necessary temperatures of 1150-1200 degrees needed to produce iron implements like nails and rivets for ship repairs. Therefore, it is clear that the Viking's explorations of North America were well-planned.

Today, a boardwalk trail connects the various reconstructed buildings and foundation sites to the Parks Canada Visitors' Centre, which also displays many other Norse artifacts found during the archaeological dig at L'Anse aux Meadows.

L'Anse aux Meadows is located 350 kilometres (210 miles) north of Deer Lake, near the community of St. Anthony. Highway 430 extends from Deer Lake to St. Anthony and L'Anse aux Meadows is located 30 kilometres (19 miles) off Highway 430 on Highway 436.

Visitors' Centre, L'Anse aux Meadows

Recontructed sod buildings, L'Anse aux Meadows

Inside sod building, L'Anse aux Meadows

Viking boat, L'Anse aux Meadows

Inside Visitors' Centre, L'Anse aux Meadows, Northern Peninsula

5

Red Bay, Labrador

The Basques

Until the summer of 1977, Red Bay, Labrador was best known for the red granite cliffs that give the bay its name. However, that changed when Dr. James Tuck of Memorial University, geographer Selma Barkham, Dr. Walter Kenyon of the Royal Ontario Museum and Arctic archaeologist Graham Rowley and his wife trampled and probed the shoreline of southern Labrador. It was Selma Barkham's dogged determination that had brought this diverse group together, culminating several years of research in archives in Europe and Canada. The most significant discovery had been a document which referred to a legal dispute over part of the cargo from a Basque ship named the *San Juan*, ripped from its moorings in a December storm and sunk in the harbour of what is now Red Bay, Labrador. Although the rocky shoals of Newfoundland and Labrador have been the demise of hundreds of ships, the *San Juan* was special, for it had sunk in 1565, making it the earliest shipwreck to be located in Canadian waters. Using sixteenth-century Basque sailing directions, Barkham was able to pinpoint numerous other sites, besides Red Bay, which were likely Basque settlement sites. And, as this expedition in the summer of 1977 was to find, evidence of early Basque occupation was almost embarrassingly obvious. A 400-hundred-year-old harpoon was found sticking out of the soil, and the characteristic red tiles of Basque architecture were found littering the ground.

Newfoundland's First Oil Boom

What had brought these early sailors 200 miles (322 kilometres) from the Basque region of Spain and France to southern Labrador? The evidence at many of the sites visited by the Barkham expedition revealed that these sailors were after whales, and in particular, whale oil. The Straits of Belle Isle seem to have be ready-made for shore-based whaling, and thousands of whales were probably harpooned and brought to shore along this coast. Although Red Bay today has a population of 350 people, it was a booming settlement four centuries ago and the largest whaling centre on Labrador's south coast. It is estimated that over a summer, its 900 residents may have brought between 180 to 200 right and bowhead whales ashore.

Once killed, the whales would be towed to shore. Near the shore, above the reach of high tide, fires would warm huge copper cauldrons which would render oil from the blubber. The rocks today are still charred from these fires, and the depressions (called *tryworks*) which held the copper cauldrons are still evident. From the pots, the whale oil would be placed in wooden 55-gallon barrels and at the end of the season, generally in the late fall, this oil would be transported back across the ocean, destined to light the cities of Europe. In fact, when the *San Juan* went down on that stormy December night in 1565, it probably held up to 1000 barrels of oil in its hold. By today's standards, this may have been worth four to six million dollars.

Red Bay Today

Visitors to Red Bay today are treated to a superb example of archaeology in action. Dr. Jim Tuck of Memorial University has returned to Red Bay every summer since the initial Barkham expedition in 1977, to continue excavations on Saddle Island and in the settlement of Red Bay itself. Starting in June and extending until early October, Dr. Tuck and his large staff dig, catalogue and restore the artifacts of the sixteenth-century Basque whalers. The group also gives tours of the research sites. Even today, evidence of the Basque presence is obvious. Whale bones are still being found around the site, and the conspicuous red tiles probably used for the tryworks roofs lie scattered on the soil's surface. Red Bay is an impressive example of a modern archaeological dig. To the visitor for whom archaeology means dusty textbooks and rows of dimly lit artifacts behind glass in a museum, a visit to Red Bay is refreshingly real and fascinating.

Red Bay, Labrador, is accessible by road from Blanc Sablon, Quebec. During the summer, a large ferry travels 40 kilometres (25 miles) from St. Barbe on the Northern Peninsula to Blanc Sablon. St. Barbe is located just off Highway 430—the Viking Trail—located roughly 300 kilometres (186 miles) from Deer Lake. Although the Basque whaling excavations at Red Bay are its key attraction, the superb salmon and trout fishing which can be found on the Forteau and Pinware Rivers also lures many tourists to the area. The L'Anse Amour lighthouse is another landmark worth visiting. It is Newfoundland's oldest lighthouse; its walls are six and one-half feet thick at the base and it stretches skyward over 100 feet (30 metres). One hundred and twenty-two steps bring the energetic visitor to the top of this castle-like structure. Close to the L'Anse Amour lighthouse is the Labrador Straits Annual Bakeapple Festival. Generally held in mid-August, this popular event revolves around the bakeapple, or cloudberry, which grows in abundance along this coast.

Archaeological dig, Red Bay, Labrador

Whale bones and tryworks, Saddle Island, Labrador

Daisies, Forteau, Labrador

6

Communities and Lifestyles

The lifestyles of western Newfoundlanders are as diverse as their environment; from the fisherman who makes his living by knowing the habits of cod or lobster to the urban dweller from Corner Brook who attends the latest exhibition at Memorial University's Art Gallery. Historically, for thousands of years, the Maritime Archaic Indians, the Dorset Eskimos and, most recently the Beothuk Indians, lived off the resources Newfoundland's land and sea provided. Today, Newfoundlanders still live off the land and sea, but in smaller percentages than in years past. A few generations ago, almost everyone fished; today, most Newfoundlanders work in the service sector. In fact, at present, less than five percent of Newfoundlanders fish for a living. In the Corner Brook area, Newfoundland's second largest community, most workers are employed in a multitude of service industries ranging from Western Memorial Regional Hospital to Sir Wilfred Grenfell College, a branch of Memorial University. Even on the Northern Peninsula, where the number of fishermen is still large, they account for less than 20 percent of the work force. Newfoundland's economy is obviously following the trend seen in most of the Western world, with urbanization and office work replacing fishing and logging as primary occupations.

Corner Brook

Corner Brook is western Newfoundland's only city. With a population of 25,000, it has all the amenities offered by similar urban centres in North America. Since it serves the entire west coast and southern Labrador, Corner Brook has many specialized services, i.e., university and hospital facilities, not typically found in small cities. The Fisher Institute of Applied Arts and Technology, provincial and federal government offices, plus a large retail trade round out Corner Brook's service sector. In addition to this, Corner Brook also relies heavily on employment from Corner Brook Pulp and Paper, a paper mill owned by Kruger Ltd. of Montreal.

Like the majority of residents who live in western Newfoundland, those in Corner Brook enjoy the outdoor recreational activities available to them. Within a short distance lies Marble Mountain, Atlantic Canada's best alpine ski area, and excellent salmon fishing can be found on the Lower Humber River. As well, hiking and cross-country ski runs exist in the eastern lakes area and Blow-me-down Mountains, and numerous sailboats ply the waters of Humber Arm throughout the summer. In mid-February, a major attraction is the annual winter carnival, which is a farewell to winter, albeit an early one, since the snow doesn't usually disappear within the city until mid-April.

Adjacent to Corner Brook is the Bay of Islands area, which was first named and chartered by Captain James Cook in 1767. Because of its scenic outports like Frenchman's Cove and Little Port, as well as its mountains and fjords, this area is gaining a reputation of being as breathtaking and beautiful as Gros Morne National Park, with many of the same features.

Stephenville

Stephenville, which was named for Stephen LeBlanc, an early American explorer, was settled in the mid-1840s. Because it is located between Europe and the United States, it was chosen as an Air Force base during World War II. Although the Air Force base was phased out in 1966, much of the architectural heritage in Stephenville today dates from this early US influence. At present, Stephenville, with a population of 10,000, provides services to for the nearby Port au Port Peninsula. Major employers include Western Community College and the Abitibi-Price newsprint mill. From a cultural perspective, Stephenville is known for its summer theatre festival, which was founded by Maxim Mazumdar. This popular festival generally runs for three weeks each summer.

The neighbouring Port au Port Peninsula is the only official bilingual region in the province, and each year Cape St. George hosts a popular French Folk Festival. The Port au Port Peninsula is almost like Newfoundland in miniature, since most of its communities are strung along the coast and its interior remains almost untouched. Its diverse shoreline is the Peninsula's biggest attraction, ranging from sandy beaches near Piccadilly to spectacular sheer cliffs at Cape St. George. The cliffs at Cape St. George are the starting point for one of the province's best coastal hikes, which traverses this rugged coastline for 11 kilometres (7 miles) to the community of Mainland.

Port aux Basques/Codroy Area

Port aux Basques, the "Gateway to Newfoundland," is the entry point for most visitors arriving from mainland Canada by ferry. As its name suggests, Port aux Basques was a port of call for Basque whalers during the sixteenth century. Today, this town provides services to the region's 16,000 people. Many workers are employed by CN Marine, which operates the ferry service to North Sydney, Nova Scotia and other Newfoundland coastal ports. The surrounding area offers outdoor recreational activities, including fishing, hiking and camping. A trek up Table Mountain provides outstanding views of the area. As well, one can view the remains of a World War II air field and radar site among other buildings. Exploriation of the nearby coastline offers numerous surprises, including a stone lighthouse at Rose Blanche constructed in the 1850s and miles of sandy beaches at Cape Ray.

The Codroy region is just north of Port aux Basques, and it is one of western Newfoundland's largest farming areas. However, its earliest settlers were sixteenth-century Basque explorers who came from the rich cod fishery. The name Codroy probably originates from cadarrai, meaning 'Cape of the King.' The Codroy Valley is shaped like a large triangle, 14 kilometres (9 miles) wide at the coast, but narrowing as it goes inland. The Little and Grand Codroy Rivers drain through the valley and are well-known salmon rivers. Today, the farms of the Codroy Valley offer a pleasing contrast to the mountains and rugged coastline of Newfoundland's south coast. The hiking trails on the nearby Long Range Mountains provide outstanding vistas of the Codroy Valley.

St. Anthony

With 3200 people, St. Anthony is the largest community on the Great Northern Peninsula. It is perhaps best known as the operation base for the medical missionary, Dr. Wilfred Grenfell. Grenfell provided much needed medical care to the isolated settlements along the Labrador coast and Northern Peninsula by building a small hospital at St. Anthony in 1905. A small museum now displays preserved photographs and other memorabilia from Dr. Grenfell's original home.

Although the Vikings first settled briefly at nearby L'Anse aux Meadows, the intrepid Basque fishermen used this coastline almost annually in the sixteenth century. It was called 'St. Anthony Haven' by Jacques Cartier during his epic voyage to Newfoundland in 1534. Although it is still a fishing community with a superb natural harbour, St. Anthony has also become an important service centre for many communities on the Northern Peninsula.

Today, the Viking site at L'Anse aux Meadows is a major attraction for tourists visiting St. Anthony, as are the nearby hiking and fishing opportunities. As well, the Grenfell Handicrafts Shop in St. Anthony displays a variety of handmade parkas, carvings and rugs produced by local artisans.

Benoit's Cove, Bay of Islands

Haying at Trout River, Gros Morne

Abandoned house, near Codroy Valley

Margaret Bowater Park, Corner Brook

Corner Brook Golf Course

First United Church, Corner Brook